Don't Drink
from the
Water Fountain

To Sarah,
I hope my poems
make you smile!
Diane Belliveau

Don't Drink
from the
Water Fountain

Middle School Poems

by Diane Belinfanti
Illustrations by Brian Hardison

Storytime Kids LLC
www.storytimekids.com

ISBN-13: 978-0-9820174-0-1

Printed in the United States of America
Book Design by Cindy Belinfanti

For my children, Aaron and Stefan,
who bring me joy and make me proud.

—D.B.

ACKNOWLEDGEMENTS

In appreciation
of Julie, Leslie, Kari,
and the students at Dodgen Middle School.

Special thanks
to Dave, Cindy and Brian
for their unwavering support and sage advice.

Contents

Test

I do my best
To pass each test,
But it is plain to see

That when I try
My answers fly
Quite far away from me.

The numbers dance
And letters prance.
They always keep me waiting.

I can't recall
One fact at all.
It really is frustrating!

With heavy sighs
I close my eyes,
Just trying to remember.

If May were here
I wouldn't care,
But it is still September!

Agenda

Has anybody read this thing? Does anybody care?
It's got all kinds of information, lots of it unfair.

Like:
Wear your pants the proper way. No food inside the classroom.
You'll need to carry your agenda just to use the bathroom!

Like:
Do not share a locker; you have got one of your own,
And don't use electronics like your iPod or your phone.

Like:
Hallways are for walking, so don't carry drinks around,
And anything left on the floor belongs to Lost and Found.

Like:
Don't be late for class or you will end up in detention.
If you do something really bad, they'll give you a suspension.

Those do's and don'ts and will's and won'ts can drive me up the wall,
And I thought school would be more fun without these rules at all.

But yesterday somebody spilled his soda on the floor.
I slipped and landed right outside Miss Johnson's classroom door.

And someone had his iPod on today in study hall.
The music was so loud, I couldn't concentrate at all.

So now I'm starting to believe that rules are not so bad,
And "Follow the Agenda" is the best we've ever had.

Undone

My book bag strap has come undone.
These textbooks weigh at least a ton!
I broke a nail. I broke a lace.
My hair is flying in my face.

At lunch I couldn't find a seat.
I didn't have a thing to eat.
Then something spilled and stained my dress.
Why do I look like such a mess?

Too many people in the hall.
I'll never reach my class at all!
I've got a minute, not much more,
Until my teacher shuts the door.

She really won't appreciate
My coming into class so late.
A few more steps—I'm very near…
OH, NO!
Is that the bell I hear?

The Dog Ate My Homework

The dog ate my homework. It really is true!
He grabbed it right out of my hands.
Then, ever so slowly, he started to chew,
Ignoring my cries and demands.
And when he had eaten the English and math
And swallowed my science and art,
He gave a long look at my history book
And greedily tore it apart.
Then just when I thought he had eaten his fill
(For how could he eat any more?)
He shredded the rest of my poetry test
And settled himself on the floor.
He lay on all fours, with his head in his paws,
And gave me a satisfied smirk
That showed from beneath very large canine teeth
The pieces of all my hard work.
I did all my homework. It really is true!
Why won't you believe what I say?
It's clear as can be what my dog did to me,
So please just excuse me today.

Marching Band

I play bass drum in marching band.
It makes the loudest sound.
It's kind of big and bulky
When I have to move around.

It's wider than my body,
And it's taller than my head.
I wish I'd signed up sooner.
Then I'd play the snare, instead.

Last Friday at the football game
I had a little trouble.
I lost my place in line
And had to backtrack on the double.

The band director yelled at me.
He blew his whistle twice.
I couldn't hear, but someone said
He didn't sound so nice.

And when the football game was done
(We lost 14 to 3)
He gave us each an icy stare,
Then pointed straight at me.

"You're always out of step," he bellowed.
"Can't you feel the beat?"
I said, "It's really hard to march
When I can't find my feet!"

Gum

Sticky, gummy,
Not so yummy,
Underneath my chair.

The floor, my shoe
And desktop, too.
It's gooey everywhere!

It seems someone
Stuck all his gum
In several hiding places.

It's plain to see
It wasn't me
'Cause I just got new braces!

Date

Anthony asked Steven,
Who asked Patti, who asked Linda,
"Would you like to go with Anthony
To Homecoming this fall?"

Linda answered, "Patti,
Please tell Steven to tell Anthony,
Thanks, but I'm already going
With a boy named Paul."

Patti passed this news along
To Steven, who told Anthony,
"Sorry, friend, but Linda
Has already got a date."

Anthony said, "I spent two months
Working up my courage
To ask Patti to ask Linda,
But I guess I'm just too late."

Anthony asked Steven,
Who asked Patti, who asked Linda,
"Can we make a date for next year?
Can you save a day for me?"

Linda said to Patti,
Who told Steven to tell Anthony,
"Next year is so far away,
But maybe—well, we'll see."

Anthony was overjoyed
When he got Linda's answer.
He said, "Looks like there's still a chance,
So I don't mind the wait."

Linda said to Patti,
"Please tell Steven to tell Anthony,
"Next year isn't looking good.
We're moving out of state."

Conspiracy

My teachers always have a way
Of giving homework every day,
And somehow they expect it to be done.

I think it's a conspiracy
To make life very hard for me.
With all this work, there's little time for fun.

They must meet somewhere secretly,
Concocting ways to torture me,
Just piling on assignments left and right.

I wish, just once, they would agree
To be considerate of me
And skip the homework, even for one night!

Nurse

Nurse, Nurse,
My forehead's hot.
Feels like I've got the flu.

I think that I'll
Stay here a while—
At least an hour or two.

Nurse, Nurse
I'm getting worse.
My throat is killing me.

It's very clear
I should be here
At least till ten to three.

Nurse, Nurse,
I can't believe
You think that I'm okay.

Please let me rest
Until my test
Is over with today!

Surviving Sixth Grade

Last year I was in fifth grade.
I was king of my domain.
I looked at all the younger kids
With arrogant disdain.

I scoffed at the fourth graders.
They seemed so immature,
And it was easy to forget
My life the year before.

But now I'm in the sixth grade,
And it really isn't fair.
The older kids all tease me
Or pretend that I'm not there.

They push me in the lunch line.
They ignore me in the hall.
And all the girls look
    down on me—
How did they get so tall?

They call me Squirt and Shorty.
That really makes me mad.
This year is turning out to be
The worst I've ever had.

I've got a million months to go
Until I reach eighth grade.
If I can just survive that long
I know I'll have it made.

The days and weeks drag
    slowly by.
I wish they would go faster.
I never knew, but it's sure true:
Sixth grade is a disaster!

New Outfit

I wore my new red shirt to school.
    It had a matching belt.
I also wore my new blue jeans
    with pockets made of felt.
So you can just imagine
    my incredible surprise
When, in the cafeteria,
    before my very eyes
Someone was wearing my new outfit,
    everything the same!
Same shirt, same belt, same jeans,
    same felt—was this some kind of game?
I tried hard to avoid her as I scooted through the door.
I didn't dare to look around, my eyes glued to the floor.
I slid into the nearest chair as quickly as could be.
The line for lunch stretched on and on as far as I could see.
I knew I ought to join my friends and get something to eat.
But I just kept on sitting there, afraid to move my feet.
I stole a glance up at the clock. Why was it so slow?
It felt like I'd been sitting there at least an hour or so.
Then, as the bell began to ring, my "twin" walked up to me.
And there we stood, identical, for everyone to see!
She said, "I think it's really neat we dressed the same today."
I tried to speak but couldn't think of anything to say.
She smiled at me and turned to go. I thought, Imagine that!
It doesn't seem to bother her that she's a copycat!
The next day I was careful with the outfit that I chose.
I wore the worst things I could find—some old, outdated clothes.
I thought, These jeans are out of style. My t-shirt isn't cool.
But I don't care, 'cause who would dare to wear
    THIS stuff to school?

Ned, Ned

Ned, Ned
Get out of bed,
And take that pillow
Off your head.

The sun is up,
The sky is blue,
And we've got lots
Of things to do.

Ned, Ned
Now you've been told.
The eggs I made
Are getting cold.

What's that you said?
You'd rather stay
Under the sheets
In bed all day?

Ned, Ned
You look all right.
Now come on down
And have a bite.

You say you have
A stomach pain?
Well, let me feel
Your head again.

Ned, Ned
You feel okay,
And now it's time
To start the day.

Ned, Ned
What's all the fuss?
Of course you didn't
Miss the bus!

There is no school,
So you can play.
Did you forget
It's Saturday?

Your uncle's here
And cousin Jake.
They're going fishing
At the lake.

Ned, Ned
You're out of bed
And dressed! Now
What is that you said?

You feel all better?
That was fast!
I guess that fever
Didn't last.

Ned, Ned
No one could tell
You weren't feeling
Very well.

Your cousin's waiting—
Time to run.
I'll see you later.
Now, have fun!

Bully

There's a bully in the eighth grade and he bothers everyone.
He teases all the girls and makes the seventh-graders run.
He always wears an angry look. His voice is loud and mean.
He's got the biggest arms and legs of anyone I've seen.
I manage to avoid him when I'm walking down the hall,
And if I see him coming I don't look his way at all.
We only share one class together—U.S. History.
As far as I'm concerned that's still one class too much for me!
He walks right by each desk and kicks our book bags with his feet,
Then gives us all a nasty stare while slumped down in his seat.
We try hard to ignore him (you don't want to make him mad),
And if he takes your pen away, well—hey, that's just too bad!
He never opens up a book. I've never heard him read,
And all the notes we take in class he
        never seems to need.
He doesn't study for a quiz
        or finish any test.
While we're all working hard he
        puts his head down for a rest.
When he's sent to the principal
        the teacher gets a breather,
But soon they send him back
        to class. They must not
        want him, either!
If I can just hang on till June
        I've got nothing to fear,
'Cause I'll be up in high school
        and he'll still be stuck
        down here!

Homework Helper

I'm looking for somebody special,
Who's got everything that I need.
I'm putting an ad in the paper,
And here's how it's going to read:

Wanted—a good Homework Helper,
Who's willing to work just for free,
Who can read and can write, is especially bright,
And is great at pretending hc's me!

My Locker

Textbooks, folders, papers, pens,
Book bag, sweatshirt, odds and ends.

Lunch leftovers from last week.
I'm afraid to take a peek.

Smelly gym clothes in a pile
(They've been there for quite a while).

Homework that is overdue,
And my science project, too.

What a mess from top to floor!
There's no room for any more.

I can get it open,
BUT
Will my locker ever shut?

Water Fountain

Don't drink from the water fountain.
  It's contaminated.
    And the cafeteria food
      Is highly over-rated.

  You'll end up with an infection
    Or the stomach flu.
      I wouldn't touch one single bite of food,
        If I was you.

    Bring your own potato chips
      And soda can, instead.
        You might get greasy fingers,
          But at least you won't get dead!

Student Council President

Student Council President
Is what I want to be.
I'm certain that position
Is the perfect one for me.

I'm very, very popular,
As everybody knows.
I have the latest everything.
I wear the coolest clothes.

My grades are pretty lousy
(I am failing math and lit),
But studying is hard for me.
I'm not real good at it.

I may not have the highest scores,
But I'm nobody's fool.
I know that making lots of friends
Is why we come to school.

I saunter up and down the halls.
The kids all wave and grin.
I don't have time to sit in class
'Cause that's not how you win.

Some Nerd decided yesterday
He'd run for office, too.
There's no way he can beat me.
He just doesn't have a clue!

I made a lot of posters
And they're hanging on the wall.
But Nerd? Well, he decided
He did not need signs at all.

We spoke at an assembly,
And I really came on strong.
I said, "When I am President
Our lunchtime will be long,

And classes will be shorter.
We'll get rid of homework, too."
A lot of people clapped for that
(Though someone gave a boo).

Then it was time for Nerd to speak.
Here's what he had to say:
"As your new President
I'll work my hardest every day.

I'll make sure everybody
Has the opportunity
To help our middle school
Become the greatest it can be.

We'll reach for excellence
In academics and in sports."
I heard a lot of students cheer.
(I think I heard some snorts).

He said, "Our students are the best.
Our teachers are first-rate.
Let's try to make this place
The Number One school in the state!"

Well, I thought that was silly.
Who cares if we're Number One?
We all just want to come to school
To have a lot of fun.

This Nerd is in for a surprise.
It's gonna hurt a lot
When he finds out he lost
Because of all the votes I got.

The votes are in and counted
And there must be some mistake.
The Nerd got one hundred and nine
While I got twenty-eight!

I just don't understand it—
How could I have been so wrong?
I really thought I'd win this thing.
I thought so all along.

I might not graduate at all.
It now seems very clear.
So I'll just run for Student Council
President next year.

New Girl

A new girl came into our class
Just several weeks ago.
She doesn't speak to anyone.
She's hard to get to know.

She whispers in a tiny voice
When someone asks her name,
And she's the last one to
    be picked
Whenever there's a game.

She comes to school quite early
And she waits beside the wall.
Her classmates, as they're
    passing by,
Don't glance her way at all.

At lunch she always eats alone
With nobody around.
There's lots of noise and laughter,
But she doesn't make a sound.

Out on the field the students play.
They tease, they talk, they yell.
But she just sits and reads a book.
She's waiting for the bell.

Each afternoon she heads
    for home
On slow and shuffling feet
And never looks to left or right,
Afraid of whom she'll meet.

The girls say she is snobby,
And the boys all think she's cool.
But I suspect she's kind of shy
Because she's new at school.

It must be hard to spend each day
Just sitting on her own,
Without someone to share a laugh
Or talk to on the phone.

At lunch I'll go and sit with her,
Ignoring all the stares.
I think she'd be quite happy
Just to find someone who cares.

For I remember being new,
So frightened and alone,
Till someone had the courage
To approach me on her own.

Tomorrow when she's
    heading home
I'll join her on her walk.
Perhaps she'll even smile at me.
Perhaps she'll even talk.

And, who knows? As the day
    is slowly
Drawing to an end,
Perhaps we'll find, both she and I,
We've made a brand new friend.

Boredom

I'm gazing out the window,
Looking at the open sky.
A gentle breeze is blowing,
Sending puffy clouds on by.

The birds outside are chirping
As they flitter to and fro,
But I am stuck inside this room
With nowhere else to go.

Each day I have to sit and wait
Inside this boring class.
My teacher's voice goes on and on…
I wish the time would pass.

Who cares about geometry,
A segment, point or plane?
If I draw one more radius
I think I'll go insane.

I'm really just not interested
In math of any kind.
If I see one more angle
I will surely lose my mind!

Outside, the world is beckoning.
It's calling me to play.
Instead, I have to be in school.
Just one more wasted day.

txt msg

lng tym no C — R U OK?
wat hpnd 2 U ystrdA?

jst 1dering wats goN on
did U hr abt sue & john?

they jst brk up last tsdA nite
I hr they hd a rl bd fite

nt a lt of ppl knw
liz and kelly tld me so

melissa saw her @ the gme
w/sum1 new — dnt knw his nme

whre R U rite nw — hstry?
I thnk tht clas is so EZ!

im brd out of my skl rite now
cuz who nds englsh, anyhow?

for rl tho, btwn me & U
my tchr dsnt hve a clu

no 1 is evN lisNng
thyr w8ing 4 the bll 2 rng

hey tim askd me out on a d8
its nxt wkd & I cnt w8!

hvnt gt a thng 2 wear
rly need 2 ct my hR

lets go shpng SatrdA
Lt me knw — is tht OK?

C U l8r — haf past 2
rly need 2 tlk 2 U

by 4 now — G2G
BFF mary jo :)

Vending Machine

Somebody's getting wealthy from our school vending machine.
Those things must be the biggest hoaxes I have ever seen.
Your dollar bill won't work if there's one teeny tiny fold,
And sometimes when you buy the candy it's already old!

Last Tuesday I lost fifty cents, and boy, did I get mad,
Especially since it was all the money that I had.
Then yesterday my chocolate bar decided to get stuck.
So there I was: a dollar short and simply out of luck.

Are these machines acquired just to give the students stress?
I really don't need soda or a chocolate bar, I guess.
But, just on principle, I think I'll give that thing a whack,
And I won't rest until I get my dimes and quarters back!

Teacher's Pet

My teacher has a favorite "pet."
He's got a special name.
And ever since he came to school
Our class is not the same.

He likes to hang out by her desk,
Her look anticipating.
He really puts on quite a show.
He's so ingratiating!

He's always making funny sounds.
It's terribly distracting.
But he is never scolded
For the awful way he's acting.

It's very hard to concentrate
Whenever there's a test,
'Cause he just paces back and forth
Without a minute's rest.

It seems no matter
    what he does
He gets her full approval.
But everyone's fed up
    with him—
We just want his removal!

He acts as if we weren't there.
His eyes are just for her.
And when she turns and smiles
    at him,
I swear he starts to purr!

I don't know what this "pet"
    has done
To earn the teacher's merit—
Perhaps I'd get an A+ too,
If I became a ferret!

Snow Days

My teacher said, "Don't think those snow days
Are Won't-Really-Have-To-Go-Days."
Finally I understand just why.

It seems some crazy kind of fool
Has stuck them at the end of school,
And now we won't get out until July!

Field Trip

We took a field trip yesterday.
It started out just great.
We planned to visit the museum,
And we could hardly wait.

We hit the bus in record time.
I got a window seat.
Beside me sat my good friend Tom.
In front of me was Pete.

We got onto the highway.
There was traffic everywhere.
We thought, With all these cars
     and trucks
We're never getting there!

We reached the city limits
When we heard an awful POP!
The driver steered us off the road.
The bus came to a stop.

"What's going on?" we all
     exclaimed.
"What happened to the bus?"
The driver gave us all a scowl
For making such a fuss.

"Hey, quiet down!" he shouted.
"Now you kids stay in your seat."
He walked around the bus
And kicked the tires with his feet.

"We've got a problem,"
     he announced
When he got back inside.
"A tire's flat." We all just sat.
Our frowns were hard to hide.

"Now, now," Miss White
     said soothingly,
"You really shouldn't worry.
We'll make a call. They'll have
Another bus here in a hurry.

We had to sit for half an hour.
The wait was long and boring.
And then, to make things
     even worse,
It really started pouring.

At last the new bus came for us.
We ran to get inside.
My clothes and hair were
     soaking wet.
(They never really dried).

The new bus driver was a snail.
Why didn't he go faster?
Tom turned to me and muttered,
"Boy! This trip is a disaster!"

It's hard to tell the story.
It is so excruciating.
The whole entire day was spent
Just hanging out and waiting.

We waited for the bus
And then we waited in the rain.
We had to buy our tickets
So we waited once again.

We waited in the lobby
And in front of every door.
The rooms were overcrowded.
There just wasn't room for more.

The dinosaur exhibit
Was the one I came to see.
(I'm kind of like an expert
In reptilian history).

I caught a glimpse of skeletons
That looked like Brontosaurus.
We elbowed people right and left,
But everyone ignored us.

Then, just as I got close enough
To see T-Rex's feet,
Miss White came in to get us,
And she hollered, "Time to eat!"

We got into the restaurant
And waited for our food,
Which made us kind of angry,
'Cause it wasn't even good.

We waited in the bathroom.
There were lines right out the door.
And when Miss White said,
    "Time to go!"
We had to wait some more.

We clambered back onto the bus.
I dropped into my seat.
Behind me sat my good friend Tom.
In front of me was Pete.

When we got back to school
There was a smile on every face.
We never thought we'd be so happy
Just to see the place.

I learned from this experience:
One thing is very sure.
Don't sign me up for field trips.
I'm not taking any more!

Silent Lunch Syndrome

Silent Lunch Syndrome
Is making me blue.
I'm lonely. I'm bored.
I've got nothing to do.

My friends are all laughing
And having a ball.
But me? I'm not having
A good time at all.

I don't think it's fair,
And I don't think it's right.
I'm feeling so awful
I can't eat a bite!

I went to the bathroom—
I just couldn't wait!
It isn't my fault
That I came to class late.

So now here I am
At a table for one.
I'm stuck in the corner
Till lunchtime is done.

If I have to eat
All alone every day,
I'll get really skinny
And shrivel away.

Silent Lunch Syndrome—
I hate every minute,
Especially now that
I find myself in it!

Pimples

It seems that every day I find a pimple on my face.
As soon as one is gone another comes and takes its place.

They always seem to choose the spots that say, "Hey! Look at me!"
Avoiding all the places that are very hard to see.

I've got a pile of pimples on the bottom of my cheek.
There's one stuck on my nose that makes me look just like a freak.

Last week I found a pimple in the middle of my forehead.
It looked all red and splotchy. It was absolutely horrid!

Mom tells me not to worry. Pimples never really stay.
She says, "Be patient. Wait a year. I'm sure they'll go away."

But one year is a lifetime when you've got a massive zit,
And all you really want to do is run away from it.

I've tried all sorts of lotions, and I've messed with make-up, too.
But nothing seems to work at all. I don't know what to do!

I might become a Dropout so my pimples can't be seen,
And then I won't go back to school until I'm seventeen!

Eighth Grade Dance

Last week in school I took a chance
And bought a ticket for the dance.
My cousin Zachary said, "Wait.
How can you go without a date?"

So, not knowing what else to do,
I thought I'd ask my good friend Sue.
She said, "I think you're very sweet,
But I'm still going out with Pete.

Why don't you ask out Allison?
She's very smart and lots of fun."
So Allison I went to find,
And she was really very kind.

She said, "I think you're awfully swell,
But I'm not feeling very well.
I've got a cold—perhaps the flu.
I feel a little feverish, too.
Isn't there someone you know,
Another girl who'd like to go?"

I asked Theresa and Marie,
But they would not go out with me.
Elizabeth, Camille and Gail—
I asked them all, to no avail.

The dance was set for Saturday.
I said, "I'm going anyway."
My suit that night looked very neat.
My new cologne smelled very sweet.

I slowly sauntered through the door
And, standing all around the floor,
Were…GUYS WITHOUT DATES, just like me!
I counted at least thirty-three.

I guess I didn't realize
There'd be so many dateless guys.
We stood around. We joked. We talked.
We watched the girls. We stared. We gawked.

I heard the D.J. say, "Last dance,"
And thought, This is my only chance.
The lights were low and very dim.
It got real quiet in the gym.

Across the room I spotted Grace.
She stood so silently in place.
She looked around expectantly,
Then turned her head and smiled at me.

I slowly walked across the floor.
It seemed to take an hour or more.
I said, "Before the night is through
I'd really like to dance with you."

I added, "This is the last song."
She answered, "What took you so long?"
We glided out onto the floor.
I'd never felt so good before.

What started as a lonely night
Had finally turned out just right.
I'll be the first one to confess,
The eighth grade dance was a success.

Girl's Bathroom

No more toilet paper.
Water on the floor.
The soap dispenser's empty.
I cannot close this door!

The paper towels are missing.
The blower doesn't work.
If they don't fix this bathroom soon,
I think I'll go berserk!

Detention

I shouldn't have Detention.
It really isn't fair.
Just because I Super Glued
My science teacher's chair.

I don't deserve Detention.
There's been a big mistake.
Just because I cheated
On a test I had to take.

I really hate Detention.
It's driving me insane!
Just because I skipped last week,
I'm stuck in here again.

Poem

I have to write a poem
In my English class today.
My paper's blank. I just can't think
Of anything to say.

My teacher said, "You've got an hour.
It doesn't have to rhyme."
But that was quite a while ago.
I'm running out of time.

How do you even write a poem?
I really can't recall.
And finding words to start with
Is the hardest part of all.

Please, someone give me an idea!
One line is all I need!
I've got to write down something
If I'm going to succeed.

The clock is ticking loudly
As the minutes melt away.
I have to speed things up here,
'Cause I haven't got all day.

I can't afford another F.
I need at least a B,
Or I won't pass this English class.
That's very clear to me.

"Time's up!" the teacher calls out,
And he rings a little bell.
I write a little faster.
Things are just not going well.

He's standing way across the room.
I think I have a chance.
Oh, no! He's walking down the aisle.
He's giving me a glance!

The teacher's heading straight for me.
My fingers start to sweat.
What happens when he finds out
That I haven't finished yet?

My head is slowly spinning
As he stops beside my chair.
He glances down and reads the words
That I have written there.

And then he says, "This poem is good.
"I really like your style."
He picks the paper off my desk
And offers me a smile.

He tells the class, "Now listen,
While I read this poem aloud."
I feel a bit embarrassed,
But I'm feeling kind of proud.

He starts to read my paper,
And here's what he has to say:
"I have to write a poem
In my English class today…"

Valentine's Day

February 14th's here.
It's the worst day of the year.
Boys buy lots of gifts to send,
While I just wait for it to end.

Girls dress up in fancy clothes,
Knowing they will get a rose.
Sometimes they get two or three,
But no one buys a rose for me.

I guess this year will be the same.
Boys don't even know my name,
And my face they just ignore.
So just what am I waiting for?

See my locker open wide,
Start to close it—what's inside?
There, beside my PE clothes
Lies a beautiful red rose.
Next to it I see a note.
I wonder what the person wrote?

"To someone lovely I admire,
Here's a rose as red as fire
Bought especially for you."
Signed, "With Love From You-Know-Who."

Wow! I got a Valentine!
I just can't believe it's mine!
Still, I wish I really knew
Who bought this rose for me—don't you?

School Bus

Woke this morning kind of late.
It's already five to eight!
Throw my clothes on, run downstairs.
Shirt on backwards, but...who cares?

Out the door and down the street.
Haven't got the time to eat.
I left home in such a rush,
I think I forgot to brush!

Belt unbuckled, laces flailing,
Back pack dragging, jacket trailing.
Five blocks never seemed so far.
Will I ever get a car?

Only seconds left to spare.
One more block. I'm almost there...

YES!
I finally reach the stop.
I'm so tired I could drop!

My poor legs are really beat.
Hope there's still an empty seat.
Yellow blinking lights I see
As the bus pulls up to me.

With a creak the doors swing wide.
Calm and cool, I step inside.
As I board the bus I say,
"What took you so long today?"

History Lesson

My teacher says that history
Is good to learn. It helps you see

What happened many years ago,
But I don't really want to know.

The battles fought on land and sea—
What's all that got to do with me?

I care about what's just begun
And not the things already done.

The dance is Friday. It won't wait,
And I don't even have a date!

Now how can I use history
To make a girl go out with me?

I wonder if George Washington,
Ben Franklin or Tom Jefferson

Had girlfriend problems just like me.
What did they think of history?

Did Lincoln always have a date,
Or did he sit at home and wait?

It might be interesting to see
If these guys were the same as me.

I guess I'll have to take a look
By opening my history book.

Bad Hair Day

Another Bad Hair Day.
That makes Number Three.
So why do these awful things
Happen to me?

I washed it this morning.
I blow-dried it, too.
I curled it. I twirled it.
What else could I do?

But still it refuses
To stay in its place.
It's flipping and flopping
All over my face.

I'm really embarrassed.
What if someone sees me?
I can't show my face.
Everybody will tease me.

Another Bad Hair Day.
I look like a fool.
I think I'll play sick
And just stay home from school.

Paper Bag

Poor brown paper bag
On the lunchroom floor,
It looks like you've been lying there
At least an hour or more.

Somebody should have told you
That it isn't really cool
To pack up all those sandwiches
And bring them into school.

Sad brown paper bag,
Feeling so forlorn,
Everybody looks at you with
Ridicule and scorn.

You should have stayed at
    home today,
Upon the pantry shelf.
Instead you came to school
And made a big fool of yourself.

Crinkled, wrinkled paper bag,
I really must confess,
You used to look so crisp and clean
But now you are a mess!

You wish that you could
    hide yourself
Under the lunchroom table.
And you'd prefer to head for home,
If only you were able.

Maybe, if you're lucky,
When they're cleaning up today
You'll end up in a trash bin,
Which is where you ought to stay.

Paper baggers, listen!
You must learn this golden rule:
Don't ever ask a paper bag
To take your lunch to school!

Gym Class

A broken lace, a sweaty sock.
Now someone hid my P.E. lock.

The walls are shaking with the noise
Of all those screaming girls and boys.

Today we're playing basketball,
A game I just don't like at all.

Each time we play, it really seems
As if I get the worst of teams.

And when the ball is thrown to me
I'm never where I ought to be.

I dribble. Then, afraid, I stop.
My fingers shake. The ball might drop.

My teammates wave. They start
    to yell.
What should I do? It's hard to tell.

The rules are mixed up in my head.
Am I supposed to shoot instead?

I take a breath and close my eyes.
I throw the ball. To my surprise

It hits the rim and settles in.
We're two points up. Our team can win!

Just then I hear the whistle blow.
The game is over—time to go.

My teammates all run up to me,
Amazed at our victory.

They lift me high into the air.
They slap my back. They yell.
    They cheer.

The coach comes up and
    shakes my hand.
I still don't really understand

Just what I did or how we won.
I only know I'm having fun.

The locker room is filled with noise
Of laughing, joking, happy boys.

I hit the showers. Then I dress.
My hair is wet, my clothes a mess,

But I don't really care at all
'Cause I just scored in basketball!

Middle Child

I'm like the Middle Child
In some crazy family.
I'm not the Baby anymore.
That's very plain to see.

I'm also not the Older Kid
Who thinks he's really cool.
And now I understand
Just why they call it middle school!

I'm trapped in seventh grade this year
With nowhere else to go,
The eighth graders above me
And the sixth grade just below.

I'm squished. I'm stuck inside a place
Some crazy kook invented.
If middle school were just two grades,
This could have been prevented!

Nobody seems to understand.
Nobody seems to care.
And life at school just chugs along
As if I wasn't there.

If I act kind of crazy
I might get someone's attention,
And then they'll have to notice me
When they give me detention!

Pop Quiz

How do you see
What the answer should be
To a question you can't figure out?

How do you study
Without a smart buddy
Who knows what the subject's about?

How do you cram
For a final exam
When you can't even focus your eyes?

How do you pass
The pop quizzes in class
When they're always a great big surprise?

Car Talk

I told my dad just yesterday,
"It isn't very cool
For me to have to take the school bus
Back and forth to school."

My dad said, "What do you suggest?
Just what would you advise?"
I cleared my throat and swallowed.
I looked right into his eyes.

"A ride to school would be
      my choice.
And I don't want to brag,
But I'd get up on time each day.
You'd never have to nag.

You go right past my
      middle school.
It's not out of your way.
You'd only have to drop me off
And pick me up each day.

And no more waiting at the bus stop
In all kinds of weather.
Besides, you're always saying
We should spend more time together.

Just think of how much fun
   we'd have.
This really could be great!
What do you say? Let's start
   tomorrow.
After all, why wait?"

My father bit his lower lip.
He shuffled and he sighed,
Then shook his head from side to side
And quietly replied,

"I see you've got things figured out.
I see you've thought things through.
But I don't think this car idea
Will work for me and you.

You say you'd always be on time.
Well, I am not so sure.
Just yesterday we had to wake you up
Three times or more!

And what if I stayed late at work
Long after school was done?
You'd have to hang around
   for hours.
That would not be fun.

My schedule's always changing,
So you can't rely on me.
Right now the school bus
Is the only option that I see.

What's wrong with riding buses?
All your friends ride buses, too.
It's really so convenient.
It's the smartest thing to do.

I'm sorry that the situation
Seems humiliating,
But I must turn down
   your request.
There's no negotiating.

Besides, in just a few years
You'll be taking Driver's Ed,
And you won't ask me for a ride
But for a car, instead!"

In Charge

If I ran the school
I would change every rule.
I would turn this place right on its head.

Every Monday would be
Weekend Day Number Three,
Leaving Tuesday through Friday, instead.

School would start right at noon
(Maybe that's still too soon?)
And we'd get out at quarter past two.

After all, we have got
An incredible lot
Of important things we'd rather do!

Every lunch time would go
For an hour or so,
With a half hour after to rest.

Homework wouldn't exist,
And we all would insist
That the teachers give only one test.

We would not need a pass
If we came late to class,
And no one would pay any attention.

We could snore. We could snooze,
What would we have to lose?
We would never be given detention!

We'd have no books to carry
(That's unnecessary),
No need for a notebook or bag.

And our folks wouldn't say,
"Where's your homework today?"
They would not have to needle or nag.

Life would really be grand
If things worked as I planned.
It would feel
Like one big holiday.

But till I run the school,
I am nobody's fool—
So I'm starting to study today!

Exchange Students

The captain of our football team walked up to me one day.

He said, "I hear you're smart in math. You always get an A.

I'm really having lots of trouble with geometry.

I sure could use your help here. It would mean a lot to me."

I was a bit surprised to hear him ask for my assistance.

Before that day I thought he didn't know of my existence!

I said, "Sure, I can help if you'll do something in return.

You're great at playing football, and I really want to learn.

You know, I'm not so good at sports. I'm never asked to play.

But maybe if you teach me I could make the team someday."

And so began the weirdest friendship I would ever know.

I taught him shapes and angles, and he taught me how to throw.

I tutored him right after school. He studied very hard.

Then he would teach me how to block and tackle in the yard.

The plan we made worked very well, much better than we'd guessed,

'Cause I could throw a football now and he could pass a test.

He finished math with passing grades (which was his greatest dream)

And I improved in football (though I didn't make the team).

The friendship that we shared together really was quite strange.

We recognized our special strengths and gave them in exchange.

He never got an A in math. I never got to play,

But we remain the best of friends until this very day.

Final Exam

Mrs. Brown told us one day,
"Students, it's already May.
June is coming, and I am
Preparing for your last exam."

All of us in English class
Said, "We're never gonna pass!
You expect us to remember
What we learned back in
    September?"

Mrs. Brown said, "You can do it.
I'll be here to help you through it.
All you really have to do
Is listen well while we review."

So each day I'd sit and write.
Then I studied every night,
Trying hard to keep in mind
Sentences of every kind.
Simple, complex and compound
Made my head spin all around.

What's autobiography?
Is it about you or ME?
What is fiction—fact or fable?
Someone help me! I'm not able!

Do these words all sound
    the same?
I forgot that poet's name!
Summary or inference?
I can't tell the difference.

Adverb, noun and metaphor—
I can't take this anymore!
All these things I can't recall.
I won't pass this test at all.

Stomach queasy, feeling scared,
I don't think I'm well prepared.
Mrs. Brown says, "Try your best.
I know you can pass the test."

She passes papers all around.
The room is quiet—not a sound.
At first I start off kind of slow,
But then my memory starts to flow.

I recognize the words I see.
Each answer's right in front of me.
I take my time and think
    things through,
Remembering from our review.

Mrs. Brown will soon collect it.
Is it too late to correct it?
I don't think I did too well.
Finally, I hear the bell!

I'm a little scared to see
What my final grade might be.
But when I come to class next day
She says, "Guess what? You made
    an A!"

Assembly

The principal is speaking.
Is he smiling? I can't see.
I'm way too busy staring
At the girl in front of me.

The faculty is cheering.
Are they getting better pay?
I'm way too busy hearing
What my neighbors have to say.

Now everyone is standing.
Is it time for us to go?
I'm way too busy sleeping,
So I guess I'll never know.

School Calendar

In early SEPTEMBER when school was brand new,
We thought, "Ten whole months? We will never get through!"

OCTOBER appeared and the weeks grew in length.
Columbus Day gave us a little more strength.

The days dragged along till NOVEMBER arrived
And, just like the Pilgrims, we barely survived!

Along came DECEMBER. Vacation was near.
Somehow we held on till the end
    of the year.

With new resolution we
    spent JANUARY
Just counting the Fridays
    until FEBRUARY.

We got a long weekend
    for President's Day,
But we knew that MARCH
    wasn't too far away.

And that was the month we despised more than ever.
Not one holiday! It just dragged on forever.

At last we reached APRIL, and with it, Spring Break.
The waiting was more than we thought we could take!

In MAY, all we got was Memorial Day,
But we didn't care because not far away

There was JUNE—only three weeks till school was all done,
And then we'd have SUMMER for nothing but fun!

About the Author

Kari Viland

Diane Belinfanti has been an avid reader and writer since childhood. She finds writing a wonderful outlet for her creative energy, drawing extensively on her experiences as a mother and educator in developing ideas for her stories and poems. Her work has appeared in several anthologies over the years. As a classroom teacher, she has gained considerable insight into the lives of students. *Don't Drink from the Water Fountain* is her first foray as a writer into the world of middle school. Earlier publications include two picture books, *A House for Miss Mouse* and *Counting on Friends*. Currently, she teaches reading and language arts at a middle school outside of Atlanta, Georgia, where she lives with her husband Dave and cat Cleo.

dbel@storytimekids.com

About the Illustrator

Brian Hardison

Always having the most fun with his pencil and paper, **Brian Hardison** has loved to draw since he was a child. He graduated from the University of Georgia with a degree in Graphic Design and Illustration and now works as a freelance illustrator in Alpharetta, Georgia. He has been involved with a wide variety of projects including book covers, advertisements, t-shirt designs, and comics. He finds inspiration from the world around him, and from the time spent with friends and family. *Don't Drink from the Water Fountain* is his second cover-to-cover book project, and he looks forward to many more.

www.altered-ego.com/brian/